AF484597

Draft - The Hollowed Dreams

F. L. Day

The Hollowed Dreams © 2024 F. L. Day

All rights reserved.

No part of this publication may be reproduced, stored in a retrieval system, or transmitted, in any form or by any means, electronic, mechanical, photocopying, recording or otherwise, without the prior written permission of the presenters.

F. L. Day asserts the moral right to be identified as author of this work.

Presentation by *BookLeaf Publishing*

Web: www.bookleafpub.com

E-mail: info@bookleafpub.com

ISBN: 9789363319806

First edition 2024

For me, as a reminder that we did it!

ACKNOWLEDGEMENT

First and foremost, I would like to thank Book Leaf Publishing for this opportunity. As soon as I saw an ad for the #TheWriteAngle Challenge, I knew that I had to apply. Getting a book of my poems published never resided in my mind, and now it has become a reality!

I would also like to extend my many thanks to the Indiana State University Writing Center, The Creative Writing Society, The History Club, and my Pruler team. All are filled with my fantastic friends and coworkers who have done nothing but cheer me on every step of the way and I can't thank them enough! While I dedicated this book to myself, this book should have also been dedicated to all of you, for without you guys, this wouldn't have happened.

I would also like to extend my thanks to many of my customers and clients who I have seen and interacted with on a daily basis and who also cheer me on. These individuals have noticed my accomplishments and have also cheered me on every step of the way, including Beth who told me that I should publish my poems into a poetry book just days before I found the ad for this challenge! Special thanks to Lisa too for reassuring me that my hard work does not go unnoticed! This means so much to me!

Finally, special thanks to my family members, who have also been there for me for the last four years of my college career. They have helped me so much with the family's genealogy and have supported my work. I am beyond thrilled to get to share this with you all!

PREFACE

Why did I write The Hollowed Dreams? I wrote them because they were all concepts that were hindering my life in some sort of aspect. While some of these poems were about pleasant dreams, others were about nightmares that haunt me.

Of course, as any other poet might suggest, I wrote The Hollowed Dreams because no one would take the time to hear about everything that has me stressed, whether it be about graduation, hoping a crush would like me back, hoping that I can make my writing journey, hoping that I'm good enough for those that I care about, etc. The list could go on and on. Regardless, my goal for this book of poetry is for other people to see that yes, I too have suffered through anxiety, depression, self-doubt, and so many other things, but I made it through these things to make it to where I am in the present moment. These poems show the reader that you can make it through the good, the bad, and the ugly, and still be okay.

And so, this is what I leave you. This book contains twenty-one memories both of wonderful dreams and horrible nightmares that you get to live through too, but it is not supposed to make you depressed while you read them, you are supposed to gain hope, insight, and resilience, exactly like I did. Therefore, I welcome you to my hollowed dreams, and I hope you get to enjoy and cherish them as I do.

All the best,

Felipe Lopez Day

The Hollowed Dreams

I walk alone in a graveyard,
I see the grave of a young soul,
And I wonder what they could've accomplished.
How painful it must be for dreams to be so
hollow.

I see the grave of a young soul,
What was their potential? What gifts did they
possess?
How painful it must be for dreams to be so
hollow,
To become nonexistent, lost to memory.

What was their potential? What gifts did they
possess?
To be marked by nothing but a lonely stone,
To become nonexistent, lost to memory.
This too could become my fate if I'm not
careful.

To be marked by nothing but a lonely stone,
And for my dreams and accomplishments to be
hollowed dreams.
This too could become my fate if I'm not
careful.
I walk alone in a graveyard.

I Can Do It, I Know I Can!

Mysteries about the future confuse me.
Yearning to be a successful writer, not for
The fame to come after me, but to
Have my vision out into the world for all to see.
I have always been a writer,
Carelessly spending hours on my perfect
manuscripts.
All I can do is keep going forward, while my
Life becomes more meaningful in this cruel
world.

I once lost my gift to a curse,
Sacrificed for my larger goals in life.

Redemption chimes into the picture,
Evaluating its next move.
Vivid colors burned into my mind.
I can do it, I know I can!
Voices call for me to keep going.
Everyone around me remains hopeful as a new
Day rolls around, bringing forth the torture.

What is Wrong With Me?

My heart thumps in my chest,
I'll walk as if I'm at my best.
I can't look into his eyes,
He smiles, and I go about trying.

I open my lips,
The word slips.
How can I tell him?
It'll tear me apart.

The words slip from my mouth,
Was it the best thing to do?
Will it be filled with endless regret?
What is wrong with me?

Did I just ruin our friendship?
Why did I have to feel this way?
There's something wrong with me.
There must be something about having a crush.

There must be something wrong with me.
I pull at my hair and scream.
Why would I think that I'd ever get
A happy ending below a rainbow?

Is there something wrong with me?
I wish I could go back in time and stop myself.
I shouldn't have said a word.
But I guess I get to live with it now.

City Boy

You talk to me, your voice
So soft, your eyes beaming.
You're probably surrounded by those city boys,
On the streets that are gleaming.

How I wanted you so badly a while ago,
And how I tried to make my move.
It didn't work for my words didn't glow,
And my game needed to improve.

How I wish you'd come down from the city
And how I wish I could meet you in the middle.
Away from them and the committee,
And far away from a stupid riddle.

I want to embrace and cherish you.
I want to meet your lips and explore,
With the hopes that we make it through.
I wish we could have that and so much more.

Faded Memories

Sometimes I walk alone at night
The headlights around me are so bright.
I can barely see in front of me,
The street lamps are too low to see.
Cars zoom right past,
Is tonight going to be my last?

When morning comes and I'm still alive,
I try to calm down by counting to five.
When morning comes, I walk in the woods.
My memory brings forth great falsehoods.
Reaching out in the country in the middle of the
day,
I find the things that I try to say.

I walk in the graveyard, the graveyard in
The middle of nowhere and I look for kin.
Why am I so burnt out?
Why am I caught in such a drought?
I've written my past out in my poems. Every
Single detail is laid out in reverie.

No graveyards, no streets, no woods,
No country, no dreams, except for falsehoods.
I look for the old and faded Memories

And I grab the gear from the armories.
I have to make it, I must keep trying
Even if the world sucks while I keep crying.

Trapped

I feel like I'm trapped in a box, stuck in the
middle of the ocean.
The wind just knocked me all over the place.
Life keeps knocking me down and I either
get the choice to stay in the Shallows or fix
myself.

I keep trying to fix myself over and over while
I just want to be stuck in slumber for five
hundred years.
Why do people start off so innocent only to end
up so cruel?
They just make me want to scream and give it
all up,
But what would they say about me?

I'm losing so much hope that I want to throw
My manuscript against the wall and scream.
I could burn it down and ditch it, or I could start
it all over
Because that's my ticket to freedom.
I have to fake it all until I get my chance to
make it.

But I keep looking at my original manuscript,
and I'm lost
In the fact that it almost ended me once before.
Was it life experience that I lacked to concoct
my characters and storyline?
I did it all for her anyway, but I've lost my own
sense of direction.
Was starting on the next story the push that
I needed to come back to square one

I can't rely on a Prince to come save me,
I don't rely on anyone, which is why I'm still
single.
I can't rely on the satisfaction from others and
Instead have to pick myself back up.

It's Always My Fault

It's always my fault.
They've told me so since the beginning.
I'm always confronted about how I
Need to change, lost to my emotions.

Would they enjoy it if I remained
A shadow stuck in the corner?
Would they enjoy it if I just became
Invisible, faded away from existence?

It's always been my fault.
I've been told since the beginning.
I'm always confronted about how I
Need to change, or lost to my commotion.

God, I'm such a monster!
I should've stopped while I was ahead.
Everything's so screwed up, and
It's all my fault.

It's always my fault.
It's never theirs.
I'm such a loser, I'm such a loser.
I'll fade into the darkness someday.

Darkness will be my new pastime,
And I'll come out of it eventually.
They'll just ask when, but I'll just say
When something's not my fault for once.

I Bet You Look Really Stupid Right Now

I bet you look really stupid right now
As I close my act and take a bow.
Are you confused as I made it somehow?

I am a man of many mysteries, but
It's no secret that I was in a rut.
Are you surprised that I made it out and that I
strut?

Did you think that I forgot about
All those times that you'd shout
And were cascaded in doubt?

I'll walk across that stage with every soul
That I've ever helped. I made their stories
whole.
I've never bowed down to control.

When trouble comes my way,
I'll put three hundred dollars on display
To show that I made it to today.

I live to make people like you disappointed.
It makes people like you feel so disjointed
As my gift has been anointed.

I'm making it, farther than you ever did.
I remember all those times that you'd say that
I'd
Just drop out of college and give up like I
always do.

I bet you look really stupid right now, huh?

Perhaps, It'll Be Better This Way

Here I am again.
Wondering why I'm here.
Wondering why I even try.
It always breaks my heart.

I ready myself for sleep and I just think,
"What would be different if I just disappeared?"
To think that my existence came
From a single wish burns in my mind.

Maybe I was sent here for a purpose
Or maybe I was sent to just be forever tortured.
What would happen if that wish never
happened?
Ha! They'd all be better off!

I send myself to the shallows in my mind,
And I cry to myself in the corner of my room.
I don't bother to look at the flames headed
In my direction. I deserve this fate.

So I'll retreat to the shallows and
I'll hang from the gallows. Sent away by my
Endless wish of ceasing to exist.
I'll go far away to where no one can hurt me.

When they inquire where I went off to,
It'll be too late. I faded away into the darkness
And I ceased to exist.
Perhaps, it'll be better this way.

I Write Poems When I'm Sad

I write poems when I'm sad,
Because the pain I feel is so bad.
I'm stuck in this endless, repetitive loop,
Why was I born into this tiny, little group?
There's a guy around me.
He's totally a sight to see.
I cower away, knowing that these feelings
Will hit me like a baseball bat.
I'm lost in the probability of possibility.
My thoughts don't have the best credibility.
So I walk away from these feelings,
Left alone to all my healings.
I feel so depressed that I want to retreat,
But my love for everyone around me has me
beat.
Destruction awakes every time I leave,
But sometimes, it needs to happen while I
grieve.

It's Moments Like These

It happened again,
Where they all misinterpret what I'm
Saying, going on to scrutinize me.
It's moments like these that
I think about my existence

It's moments like these that I
Imagine myself alone in a graveyard,
Where no one can talk to me, and I remain
Silent for its duration.
Why is it so hard to be around people?

I walk by the graves of the dead,
And I ponder about their lives.
Were any of them socially awkward like me?
Did any of them have friends who
Dissociate with them when they joke?

It's moments like these that I want
Nothing more than to fade into the darkness, for
The darkness feels like home after a while.
I can sit in the corner and not be bothered,
At the end of the day, that's where they want me.

I used to proclaim that I'd rise like the dead,
Or that I'd relish with the man of my dreams.
I used to stand firm in my beliefs and
I used to be kind, as it was what I was taught.
It's moments like these, I think about how I am
such a fool.

It's moments like these when they
don't even see that I should have stayed alone.

Our Words are Our Last

"I will rise again, like the dead"
or I won't, you'll never know.
I'm always meant to be filled with dread.
Darkness comes around whenever I sew.

They once said I'd never amount to anything,
Even when I tried to do my best.
My gift was never going to bring
The big bucks or be the best.

Someday, they'll wonder where I went,
My words left all bent.
My tombstone will be broken,
Each piece will be your token.

My words were lost to the flames,
The flames of lost desire.
No one will ever be the blame.
My fangs shall never sire.

So let's get lost, lost in the woods,
Let's never look back at the past,
and instead, look out in hoods,
Hiding our faces as our words are our last.

Eva

Eva writes poems and stories,
Keeping track of her great inventories.
She loses track of time,
Always writing her way through grime.
Her peers always cheered her on,
Always questioned by her loved ones
Who she tried to keep them together,
But they'd always break the tether.

Always inquired about her future,
And they'd always leave a great suture.
Regardless of her accomplishments, they'd
always
Look down, sending her words off to the blaze.
They think they sit above her, all
High and mighty, but cower when she'd call.
Eva never cared. Who were they to throw
judgment?
She'd have the last laugh with misjudgment.

They never listened to her, disregarded her,
And left her feelings down to a blur.
Trying to shrug off the concerns to remain
bashful.
Always trying to remain calm, not trying to

Be lost in thought of being the disappointment.
She's left to keep going, like rubbing an
ointment.
She'll have to see this all through.

Eva lost herself in trying to be so
Perfect to all around her. Trying to go
Be the perfect relative to all,
But her own self-worth came to call.
Why should she be judged?
The lines are about to be smudged.
She never disappointed anyone, they
Disappointed her instead. There will be a day

Where she'll win,
And where she'll begin
Again, it won't matter
Who decides to chatter.
Eva will continue on and
It won't matter who is gone,
Because she writes books when she's sad,
And those who have wronged her can stay mad.

Goodbye Darkness, hello depression,
You're not gonna cause her regression.

Don't Blink

You're never gonna go anywhere,
You're lost in your own desires.
Get a grip and move on.
You've got work to do.
They never cared anyway.

Let me be lost in the darkness,
Don't attempt to pull me back.
They say it was my fate all along,
And not one was supposed to see me here.
Don't blink, for you've already missed me.

In a decade or two, maybe even three,
They'll wonder what happened to me.
But they won't find him.
He won't be buried in a cemetery,
Or found with the living.

They'll ponder what happened, but
All they'll see is a trace gone cold.
They don't know it yet, but he will
Be gone because I took his place.
I killed him, and I remain.

This chapter ends, and it will never be continued
It was buried away after
Being locked away behind the ink.
He won't be there, he's long gone by now.
What remains is far from dead, though.

Eclipse

Don't look up at the sun.
Wait for the darkness to come,
And take it in for all that it gives.
Look up at the sun and count your blessings.

And when darkness captures the ground below,
Keep in mind all of the obstacles
That you went through to get here.
Look up at the moon and take it in.

And when the darkness gives way to the light,
Don't be left wanting more,
But be happy that the moment came and went.
Smile that you were caught up in the darkness,

But don't let the darkness overpower you.
An eclipse will only last a few minutes,
But darkness can last for decades.
Don't let it be a timeless classic.

Don't let the darkness determine your death,
But instead, let it empower your life.
Don't spend time thinking that this will
Never happen again in your lifetime.

For an eclipse happens within us all,
But continue to be as happy as a four
Leafed clover, and we take in the happy
memories.
For that is our very own timeless classic.

Our lives aren't meant to last forever,
But the stories we leave will
Never get to breathe that one word.
They will never get to say adieu.

The Sunset

There's never a competition between us,
But you decided to be competitive in
Our silly little games.
I watched you walking down the hall,
But I never stopped to say, "Hi."
That changed when you let me
Borrow a pen in class and how
I clung to it like it was the bringer of a perfect
life.
You made the semester better.

On a chilly fall day, when we had
Hung out under the trees, you'd whisper
In my ear, "Let's go watch the sunset."
We went up to your dorm room, and we
Sat by the window, looking at the horizon,
But I'd always break my glance
To look at you, hoping you'd kiss
Me under the beautiful sunset.
You'd ask if it was beautiful, and I
Said, "Yes, but not as beautiful as you."

We grew distant after a while,
And you surrounded yourself with the city boys
While I was in my room getting

To know Orwell, Austen, Milton, and
Shakespeare.
At the end of the semester, you
Never said "hi" again, and I couldn't
Help but wonder if it was something I
Did to you. Lost in my own
Direction, lost in the words.
Why did we have to be so different?

Graduation was approaching, and I
Walked with the knowledge of
Morrison, Fitzgerald, Hughes, and Poe.
Why was I unable to draw you in?
Do I need to write poems like
Dickinson, Whitman, Yeats, or Teasdale?
Time was running out, and you watched
Me on the graduation stage.
I accept my diploma, proud to be
Armed with all that I've worked for.

Twenty years later, you revisited campus,
And I ran into you, you who brought
Your kid is here to tour the campus.
Are you trying to win me over again?
You tell me that you have a job now,
Unrelated to your degree, but here
I am with a Doctorate in English,
Unphased by your antics,
And instead, led by my career,

And I enjoy the sunset with my husband.

After all these lonely years,
I found the perfect man, one who knows
All that have trained me.
I walk away from you, and I return
To him, where we can watch the sunset
Together.

The Day is Ending

The day is ending.
The sun is setting.
The birds are chirping your name.
I jot down my final thoughts on paper,
And I write your name in beautiful ink.
Why did I not say goodbye to you when
I had the chance?

I place my rough draft on the table, and I
Scurry to the kitchen to cook up a meal.
I am leaving tomorrow, and you shall
Never see me again.
It makes me feel so hollow,
Exactly like the lost dreams that
I wrote about while I was thinking of you.

Our fates were just never meant to meet,
And we were never meant to be.
We could have been two gay men tied together,
But now I realize that we are supposed to be
Two gay men living two separate lives.
And so tomorrow,
I'll get in my car and drive down the highway

Your name will echo in my head the entire drive,
And I will lose myself in what could have been.
I'll get over this eventually for
The day is ending,
The sun is setting,
And my feelings will run out.
A few years later, we'll just forget about each
other,

Unless you stumble across a book
In a bookstore, and it has my name on it.
Your thoughts race as you go to pick it up.
"Can it be? Is it him?"
The name is so unfamiliar that you look at
The back cover and see my picture there.
Only then, will you remember me.

It seems all that hard work
Has been turned into a book of art,
Art that has your name etched in
It's words, a name that I had long since
forgotten.
I told you that we'd forget
While you now remember,
My memories are now hollow.

I Wish I Could be Apathetic

I've got so much on my
Mind right now, it's pathetic.
It makes me want to cry,
I wish I could just be apathetic.
I threw away my old memories,
Bound with my old accessories.

It'll be better this way,
All that clutter took up my room,
But emotions try to sway
Like the cold feet of a groom.
Who am I without these things?
I feel like a wedding with no rings.

I wish I could just be apathetic,
It'd make things easier,
But I'm so sentimental that it's pathetic.
These dreams are acting so sleazier.
I feel like I've been removed from six feet under,
My gold and riches are there to plunder.

My childhood is dead,
And I'm now lividly living.
It fills me with great dread,
While I'm giving

My all.
All of this stands too tall.

I know I'm not dead yet.
My childhood is, though.
I'll be living with great regret,
I'll freeze like I'm buried in snow.
I wish I could just be apathetic,
But then again, that would only be pathetic.

The Writer's Room

All my life,
I've felt like I've been stuck
In the same place, at the same time.
Always told that this disaster was my fault,
That it's my ambition that's the greatest waste.
It's the fate of the writer's room.

I could write about a boy who battles
with depression or about a gay love story.
I could write about a boy who is so gifted
Or I could write about my darkest thoughts.
It's my ambition that makes me deal
With the fate of the writer's room.

Why am I always looked down upon?
Like my gift is just a waste of time,
And that I'm just not meant to dream.
What's the point of continuing,
If a person is not allowed to dream.
Is that the fate of the writer's room?

I once wrote to get even,
And to heal from all my losses.
I wrote to stay sane,
So I wouldn't be tempted to drive behind
A log truck on the highway.

Is that the fate of the writer's room?

I once wrote to distract my mind
From the vultures of my neighborhood.
Now I have to protect what's mine
Behind a battlement of purple paint.
Is this the fate of the writer's room?
Must I stay in seclusion for the rest of my days?

It's okay though, they'll just say I'm a poet,
That I grew up to be a crazy and cranky old
man.
That all my life led up to this little state of mine,
Away from the light, and captured
Under the darkness that is my life.
Is this the fate of the writer's room?

All my life, I've been in the writer's room,
Stuck in the same cycle over and over again.
All my life, I've been in the writer's room,
Hoping that I could meet a man just as crazy
As me, living a life in seclusion, in the hills.
That would be the perfect writer's room.

And when my daughter grows her own
Ambition, I won't be the one to clip her wings.
And when my son decides that he wants
To be a trailblazer, bringing forth the new age,
Who am I to stop him?

They'd be the outcome of the writer's room.

And when my grandchildren inquire about
The books on my bookshelf.
They can be proud to see the consequences of
The writer's room,
And perhaps it could run in the family,
The writer's room transcends a single room.

We gather around the kitchen table,
And my granddaughter finally grabs
A book from my hollowed bookshelf.
Are these the hollowed dreams I left behind?
They'll gather around her and they'll smile,
Because they are what remains,

They are stronger than any book I made.
Why did the others not see his ambition?
Why did they not let him dream?
There are so many questions that will
Be left unanswered. It's the greatest mystery,
But they are what remains.

Is this the fate of the writer's room?
It isn't yet, but it could be eventually.
If that's not the fate, then what is?
The fate of the writer's room is in shambles,
And though I've been told it is my fault,
It's not yet, but it could be.

As long as my heart beats,
And as long as I still function,
The fates may never be known to you.
I may stand brokenhearted, and
Depressed as hell, I know that this feeling
Is only temporary, and it will pass.

These feelings are my dreams that feel so
hollow,
And my family will sit and ponder, thinking that
I'm just a mad man and that I'm just
"Depressed and negative all the time."
Little do they know, that I'm as positive
As I've ever been, and my dreams will live.

For as long as I keep writing,
My dreams will never cease.
Etched in my memory, are these
Fallen memories, all almost lost to time,
Forever immortalized, for the world to see.
And is that the fate of the writer's room?

No. It's not.
The writer's room hasn't even been built yet,
But once it is finally built,
No one shall tear it or burn it down.
And the humble beginnings reside in my heart.
That is the fate of the writer's room.

2024!!

In front of me stand
Two rough drafts.
They both could be the perfect brand,
Intricately plotted out like perfect grafts.

They look back at me and I admire them.
The next steps are going to be so rough,
But they won't take place postmortem,
For this Writer's heart is too tough.

I used to be a shadow in the corner,
But remaining in the darkness isn't my style.
Even if I'm dragged off to the gallows,
I'll live my life with a full smile.

Like an accomplished newsman,
I smile and I close my computer.
I stand stronger than death and his loves,
And past the days of finding the perfect suitor.

Don't be mistaken, I've had a blast.
I've walked the bridge of the dead,
And the words I've written will never be my last.
I was never created from the perfect molds.

Regardless I'm still the greatest piece of work,
And I've concocted the greatest lore.
For now, I'll walk across that stage with a smirk,
And we'll party like it's the end of 2024.

Finale

"Honey, why don't you sit back and drink a
glass of wine?"
So I shall.
You say, "Honey, what exactly is on your
mind?"
And I shall say that I have a class coming up.
You say, "Is that all?"
I'll say that I also have certification tests coming
up.
"Honey, you stress far more than anyone I know.
There's more."
I'll say that I'm planning four books,
planning three novels, and I am working on a
fourth book that's a mystery.
You'll say, "Well, why is it a mystery?"

I'll say that it's because I talk about my two
manuscripts so much,
That this gives me the one thing to plot in the
background,
Constantly teasing those who know me that
something is coming.
And you'll say, "Okay, okay. I get it. What else
troubles you?"

I'll say that I also have student teaching coming up.
"Is that all?"
If I said that it was, would you stop asking?

You'll say, "Honey, I know you're going through a lot right now."
And I'll nod with tears in my eyes. Sure, I did this to myself,
But I also need this, this that gives me something to live for.
You'll say, "Honey, I feel like you're just down all the time.
What makes you happy?"
What does make me happy?

I want to be successful, I want to be the light in the darkness,
And I keep writing until I can't write anymore.
You inquire about my books, but I keep my mouth shut,
For secrecy is my only treasure,
While my brain keeps thinking,
What if I die before I get to accomplish success?

That's the thing though, patience is the only thing that
Leads to success.

You say, "Honey, I know you've been doing a
lot, and while
You think that no one notices your hard work,
You're wrong, because I noticed, and people
noticed."
Tears swell up in my eyes, and I can't even wipe
them away.
I say that means so much to me,
Because it does. My summer has been filled
with
Torture, lacking the visitation of the cemeteries
that
Held the family members that I once studied.

I hit Dean's List last semester, while I narrowly
missed it
The semester before that, and for someone to say
that
They've noticed that I've worked my ass off to
make
A difference and a life for myself, makes me feel
so accomplished.
So many people around me, many of whom I see
on a daily basis have
Been rooting for me this entire time, and I failed
to see that.
While I capture the torture and the love in my
writing,

I almost forgot about my own soul in the
process.

I can't even begin to think about the goals I have
down the road.
You ask, "What are they?" and I reply that I
want
To walk across that graduation stage, not only
bringing light to
The next generation, but I worked hard to get
there.
I tell you about publishing my novels someday,
hoping that
My stories can reach those who have suffered
like we suffered,
And those who have loved like we get to love.
I tell you about how I want to change my name,
ridding myself
Of the legacy of a deadbeat father, hoping to
instead forge a new
Legacy that echoes not only those who came
before me, but
Also, every single person in my own family,
who I hope I
Have made proud in some form or fashion,
hoping that they
Know that I've been doing my best, far more
than what was
Ever once expected of me.

These are The Hollowed Dreams, these are the
dreams that
I have clasped onto with the hope that resides in
what remains
Of my heart.

I've felt so trapped, always feeling that
everything was my fault,
Hoping that those who have doubted me every
step of the way are
Feeling really stupid right about now.
The sun is setting, the stories are almost over,
and 2024,
A year of misery and suspense will be almost
over as I
Accept my diploma.
These are the faded memories that will reside in
my mind,
And at the end of the day, these hollowed-out
dreams
Will be the very beginning of my truest career.
I stopped being a shadow.
I am stronger than death and his loves,
And instead of walking on the bridge of death,
I instead walk before you as a newly published
poet.

And while I am building this universe from the
ground up,

I am not doing it for the fame or for the honor,
But instead am proving it all to myself,
Because I can do it, I know I can.
While a simple thank you will never cut it
For everyone who has stood by my side for this
entire time,
The Hollowed Dreams,
Will never be hollowed again.